HOW TO IMPROVE MEMORY FOR KIDS, TEENS AND YOUNG ADULTS

LEARN HOW TO REMEMBER THINGS FASTER, HOW TO PERFORM and SCORE HIGHER IN YOUR NEXT TEST/EXAMS, HOW TO USE DIETS TO IMPROVE YOUR MEMORY

SCOTT LEWIS &E.D Jonas

2

COPYRIGHT

Copyediting and proofreading by jonasGroup.

Book design and composition by D' PROFF printing, Flora Printing Press

3

TABLE OF CONTENTS

4

5

INTRODUCTION

We learn to remember, and not to forget. Of what benefit it is to store pieces of information in our memory, but only forgets them at most crucial time of our lives? Have you read for an examination or interview as a student, but suddenly forgot what you have stored in your memory within a twinkle of an eye? Have you ever been asked a question that you literarily know the answer to, but couldn't provide the simple and smart answer? Or do you forget people's name, addresses and phone numbers at the worst moment?

If you are a victim to this or you have ever been, you would need memory improvement to keep your brain working and active again. An Irish proverb said, "May you never forget what is worth remembering, and may you never remember what is best forgotten." You'll need sound memory to store important information.

Whether you are 3 years old or 75 years old, it is still possible to work on your memory and remember anything at will. It doesn't matter your age, status, race or sex, with discipline and right approach you can improve your memory through meditation, brain exercise, games and diets. Henry Ford said, "Whether you think you can, or you think you cannot, you are always right." Therefore, open your mind to all possibilities. Truly, anything is possible to him that believes.

In this book, you will learn different methods and techniques for:

- Memory improvement.

- How to practice meditation.

- Mind mapping techniques.

- How to score and perfume better in your next semester examinations.

- How to boost your brain power.

- List of 25 natural foods that can help to improve memory. *Because, if athletes have always eaten to win, we too can use food to improve our memory.*

Therefore, welcome on board and let's rock the boat together as we work toward, having a better and improved memory functions.

Scott Lewis

10

CHAPTER ONE

WHAT IS MEMORY

IMPROVEMENT

By definition, memory is the ability to recall information about past events, the ability to think, retain and make plans for future events. Have you ever walked into your living room with intention to pick something, and suddenly forgot what exactly you were looking for? Have you ever been on a search for your room key, car key, glasses, or toothbrush and other things that we commonly keep at particular place in our homes? Why do we often forget things that we literally know about? Does it mean we have poor memory, short memory or we just need a memory improvement?

In fact, we all have troubles remembering things. But it is more common amongst children and teenagers to forget what they've recently learned. Some adults on the other hand easily forget things due to distractions, because they have little or no time to remember things.

Children and teenagers easily remember things like-phone numbers, names, items and where things are kept than adults. Honestly, no human has perfect memory. We often forget things that are irrelevant, but once important information are forgotten so easily, there might be need for memory improvement. Memory involves learning, retaining and remembering information. There is a strong connection between the brain and our senses (Taste, touch, vision, small and hearing) which helps in receiving and recording information. It is important that vital pieces of information are recorded in our brain, because information not recorded, cannot be recalled or memorized.

There are basically two types of memory: - Short memory and Long memory.

SHORT TERM MEMORY

Short memory is the ability for us to remember or recall something that we recently heard or saw and can only last for about five (5) seconds. Information contain here are easily forgotten because they are not memorized and recorded in our brain.

One Sunday evening, I was invited to a friend's marriage anniversary. On my arrival, I was given a key-holder as present. Immediately I got home, I attached my car key to it and dropped it at my usual spot. When I woke up the next morning to resume work, I took the key holder and hooked it to the belt loop of my pant (trouser). Few minutes later, I thought I had misplaced the key. I searched for it in every corner of my living room, but couldn't find it. After the rigorous search, I finally sat to think of the places I had been to – the toilet, kitchen and dining. Soon after, I realized that I had a new key-holder fixed at the belt loop of my pant to which the car key was attached. Gosh, "How could I have forgotten that I have a key-holder fixed to my belt loop?" I said to myself.

Then, I realized that, our brain is programmed to function in certain ways. We need to train our brain to retain and recall certain information. Just imagine if I had decided to think about that situation in the first place, I would have saved time, energy and get to work on time. It finally took me several days to record this new act in my memory. We need to train our brain continually, to retain new information about things we have recently learned, heard, saw, or acquired, in other to replace our old ways of learning and getting things done.

Teenagers and young adults might need to practice, learn, and memorize lessons/things before it becomes recorded in their memory. Although we learn at different pace, there is need to practice things we have recently learned, for better and improved memory even though you consider yourself a genius.

LONG TERM MEMORY

Long-term memory: This focuses on the ability of the brain to recall information that had been stored in the past. You need to continually repeat the information, or visualize it, so that it becomes recorded in your brain for quick remembrance. It may take long time to forget information that had been recorded in the brain. The advantage of long-term memory over short memory is that, it has no limit to the amount of information it can store.

Although, our brain has the ability to grow new cells as we age, its ability to process, and the speed to recall information becomes slow. Because, the older we get, the more information we are exposed to, and the lesser we are able to recall certain memories. In this modern society where teenagers and young adults are exposed to things we never knew, even when we were in age 30s and 40s, distraction from learning, increases everyday amongst teens. Therefore, there is need to pay attention to things that are important to enhancing learning experience. As a teenager or young adult, when learning a new course or studying for an examination, it is important to avoid distractions and interruptions, then, concentrate and pay attention on the course or subject matter. Because attention is all you need to improve your memory retention. The ability to pay attention and listen during learning process is the core difference between intelligent students and average students. I don't dispute the fact that, some people are more intelligent than others, but your ability to concentrate and pay attention to what you've been taught, will enhance your memory retention and the ability to recall stored information. If you or your child didn't do pretty well in your last semester examinations, there might be need for a "memory shift" - so that hours spent, playing computer games and other stuffs can be reduced and refocused into academic learning through visualization, organization and association. As pupils, students, or parents, if you desire to score above average in your next test, you will need to practice "The 10,000 – Hour Rule," if you are not a genius. *The rule states that you'll need about 10,000 hours of practice to become exceptionally good at a skill.*

Now, if we do simple mathematics of the above rule, you will find that it takes about 417 days to become exceptionally good at any skill. As student with average grade, you will need about 3 hours of uninterrupted studies daily, six days a week, to come out of your average class. But if you are a lower grade student, then, you will need to put in more efforts and attention to your studies in other to join the middle grade class.

How to Improve Memory and Concentration in Teens and Young Adults During Studies

"May you never forget what is worth remembering, and may you never remember what is best forgotten"- Irish Quote

As students, summarizing a whole semester lesson note onto few pages of paper during examinations requires good memory. Information can either be stored for short-term purposes or long-term purposes. Realistically, you need a short-term memory to record information when preparing for examinations.

Have you ever imagined why we often forget answers to questions we attended to during exams few months, weeks, days, or at worst, hours after taking part in the exams? It is simply because, the information was recorded in the brain for short-term purpose, and this experience shows the relationship between learning and psychology.

To improve information retention as teenagers or young adults, it is important you do the followings during studies:

(1) **Write important Notes**: Note taking has a way of improving child's retention ability. But in this modern and digital world, where Notepad, ipad and e-learning materials had almost taken over our old method of writing and learning, it is now difficult to ask teens and young adults to write notes during studies. If using ipad and other e-learning materials is your preference, then, it is important that you type important points in your notepad or computer. This method is as effective as writing notes with pen and paper.

(2) **Discuss the points you have noted with friends, colleagues and classmates.** There is power in discussion, because information shared or discussed with friends and associates are not easily forgotten. *In my school day, I was never a genius. I was an average student who would need to practice and recite important notes severally, before it ever became recorded in my memory. On the other hand, I had a roommate (Anthony) who would need to hear or read something once, and it glued to his brain. Why I would spend about three (3) hours to memorize a note,*

Anthony would only need about 45 minutes to memorize same information. So, I noted that, I needed more time to work on my memory retention than Anthony.

Sometimes, nights or days before my examinations, I would discuss some important points recorded in my study note with Anthony and few other friends. Eventually, if questions are set from the areas I discussed with friends, then I would leverage on our conversation to provide answers to the question asked. This "studies secrete" helped me to score above average in my final examinations. As parents, you can help to discover your kid's memory retention, by asking them to tell you important points or discussions you had with them few minutes back, hours, day, or months as the case maybe to test their memory retention ability.

(3) **Improve learning through play**: Naturally, the human body hates work and loves play. If the process of learning and studying isn't made fun and interesting, kids and teens may liken it to work. Again, kids and teenagers learn through play which helps to intensify learning experience. You or your child

can get involved in the following brain exercises to improve learning:

(i)   Take a break for about five (5) minutes and walk round your study's room, while reciting important points you have written.

(ii)   During studies, you can take a deep breath and hold it for few seconds, and then breathe out. This exercise helps to improve memory and controls emotion.

(iii) Play cards and puzzle games: Games like Uno, chess, scrabble, and Go fish, can help to improve memory. For example, when playing Chess, you will need to play by the rules, get involved in solving problems, plan and finally coordinate your actions against your opponent. These activities require big deal of memory function. Hence, they can help to improve working memory in teens and young adults.

(4) **Listen to Good music**: Playing your favorite music at a low tone during studies can boost your mood. This shows the relationship between learning, and emotion. When your mood is boosted,

your productivity level becomes high and your ability to assimilate and retain information increases. So, when next you are studying for a new course, and it seems difficult to comprehend, use this secret weapon to overcome.

(5) **Visualize information you have retained in your memory**: There is an old adage that says, "A picture saves thousand words." Your ability to visualize information recorded in your brain, and put down in the form of picture or diagram will help to recall it

when needed (especially for examination purpose.)

(6) **Engage in continuous practice:** "Practice makes perfect". Repeated practice helps to improve information retention in our brain. Teens and young adults may not easily forget things they've practiced severally.

(7) **Use scent (perfume or rose flower) to improve your memory:** Smelling the rose or using other nice smelling perfume can help to boost your mood, improve relaxation and increase

focus which in turn helps to improve memory.

(8) **Avoid drinking alcohol**: Heavy consumption of alcohol can bring the teen's brain to a critical stage. *I wouldn't forget in hurry, what happened a certain night in my college days. I had a mathematics test to write the next day, but during my study hours in the night, I discovered that I was under stress, and my brain couldn't assimilate what I was studying. I talked to a friend about it and he said "let us go and have a drink to open your brain." Oh yeah! I felt excited,*

and we went to a close bar, I drank just a bottle of beer and returned to my study room in anticipation to download the book into my memory. Surprisingly, I started falling asleep, my stress level got increased, and I could feel my brain cells sleeping already even though my eyes were opened. Suddenly, I bowed my head on my reading table and fell asleep. I woke up the next morning feeling emptied in my head. Then, I decided to take a shower and rushed back to my study room to start over again. Finally, I got what I deserved in the examination hall. That would be a story for another day. Although this may not happen to everyone, but heavy consumption of alcohol, contributes to memory loss in many cases.

HOW TO IMPROVE MEMORY FOR LONGER RETENTION

1. **Use Rhymes and Rhythms to improve your memory**: The power of rhymes and rhythms in recitation cannot be over emphasized. This is the

reason; we are able to recite few things we were taught even in our elementary and primary school. Now, just close this book for a moment and recite something you were taught in your elementary school. For me, I am able to remember and recite the "twinkle, twinkle, little stars".

2. **Learn to Chunk words/numbers**:

Chunking does not only improve memory in kids, teens and young adults, it also helps adults to develop better memory retention. Now, try to remember six (6) telephone numbers without going through your phone contact. How possible it that? To some of people, this might be a big deal. To help improve memorization in kids, teens and adults, always try to divide given items, numbers, or words into small group(s). For example, if you are to memorize 2022448670, it may be easier to remember if it is grouped as 20-22-44-86-70. Words like INFORMATION can be grouped as In-for-ma-tion, EXCELLENT as Ex-cell-ent, – these little tricks can help to improve working memory.

CHAPTER TWO

WORKING MEMORY

Working memory refers to the ability to hold and make use of short-term information recorded in the brain while performing other tasks. Children and teens are able to hold on to certain pieces of information why performing other tasks. But, children and teens suffering from Attention Deficit Hyperactivity Disorder (ADHD) may have difficulties remembering things, when they are engaged in multi task activities. Amanda Morin in her post "8 working memory boosters" Asked? "Does your child have a hard time keeping one bit of information in mind while doing something else? If he is helping make spaghetti and the phone rings, does he forget he needs to go back and keep stirring the sauce? If he often has trouble with such tasks, he might have working memory issues". As parents, if you've observed that your child forgets things so easily that he should literarily remember, there might be need

to caution his action.

HOW TO IMPROVE WORKING MEMORY

We can improve working memory in teens and

young adults by following the steps listed

below.

(1) **Create and use To-Do list**: *The*

worst method to preserve information is

to store it in the memory, while the best

way to keep information is to write it

down. Whether you believe or not, the brain has the tendency to forget vital information even at critical time. Information recorded in the brain and also written down is easier to recall, than the ones just memorized. Make sure you have a To-Do list of important things you would do in school, home, or workplace the next day or so. As this method has proven to be the most effective way of keeping information. How often do you remember the password to your Gmail account, Paypal account, Yahoo, Pinterest, Facebook, Twitter and other social networking platform? There is need, to keep them safe in your dairy for quick and easy access.

(2) **Assign a place to keep important items**: To avoid the embarrassment of searching for car key, house key, children's school bag, lesson notes, sucks, school sandals/shoes, make conscious effort to keep items at particular place in your home/office. It often gets me angry to see my wife (Sarah), searching and asking the kids, where are your school bag? Shoes? Or pen? When they are already prepared for school in the morning. This situation can

be avoided by keeping items in particular

place or by asking your kids to do same.

(3) **Get involved in brain exercise:** The

interesting thing about brain exercise is:

(i)   It challenges you to take new

action.

(ii)   It teaches you something new.

(iii) It gives you the opportunity to

learn new skills you can build on.

(iv) It is rewarding (because it helps to

improve memory.)

To practice brain exercise, learn new things you

have always anticipated for. Examples, How to

speak a foreign language, How to play piano, violin, guitar, How to dance tango, How to play golf, tennis, basketball or anything you have always wished to do. The best time to start is NOW!!!

In summary, the following tips can help to improve memory in teens and young adult.

i.   Engage in brain workout.

ii.   Engage in light physical exercises like aerobic exercise.

iii. Discuss important facts you need to remember with friends.

iv. Avoid stress (specifically in exams period)

v. Use laughter to boost your mood.

vi. Eat healthy meals.

> ## *Tips on memory improvement for all ages*

i. Organize new information in an easy way.

ii. Brainstorm the new idea or information received.

iii. Visualize information either in picture or diagram.

iv. Practice new idea you have learned.

v. Engage in meditation.

vi. Take supplements and vitamins to boost your brain power.

vii. Get enough sleep in the night if your day was stressful.

viii. Chew gums and use scent to boost your mood.

CHAPTER THREE

MIND MAPPING

Mind mapping is one of the effective ways to improve memory amongst teenagers and young adults. It involves the concept of visualizing information in other to make connections to link different pieces of information together as a single unit. It is a note taking technique that fits in pieces of information together in various ways. Mind mapping is an effective method when:

a.   Solving problem (mathematics, physics and general)

b.   Studying for examination

c.   Writing essay

d.   Creating presentation

e.   Making notes.

HOW TO DRAW SIMPLE MIND MAP

1. Write the title of the subject at the centre page and circle it.

2. Use arrows to connect subtopics to the main title.

3. Draw circle round the subtopics and make them smaller in size.

4. Connect further other important points to the subtopic using arrows.

5. For additional keyword or fact, connect them to the relevant heading or subheading.

For example, here is a simple mind map design for a book title, "Memory Improvement"

50

Age

Alcohol

Imagination

Factors affecting
memory improvement

Meditation

How to improve memory
mmemory

Principles of
memory Improvement

Memory improvement

Mind
mapping

Causes of poor memory
improvement

Working
memory

Depression

Grief & Death

How to improve
working memory

Note:

i.   Use different font size for topics and subtopics

ii.   Use symbol and images to represent words

iii   Use different colors to separate ideas

iv   Use arrows to link points together.

Factors that influence memory process:

Aman Sharma in her article, "*11 factors that influence memory process in Human*" listed the following points.

(1)   Ability to retain

(2)   Good health

(3)   Age of the learner

(4)   Maturity

(5)   Will to remember

(6)   Intelligence

(7)   Interest

(8)   Over learning

(9)   Speed of learning

(10)   Importance or meaningfulness of the material

(11)   Sleep or rest.

HOW TO IMPROVE MEMORY

WITH MEDITATION

Meditation changes the physical structure of the brain positively by improving attention, memory, and sharpens one's ability to focus. A study in Journal Consciousness and cognition revealed that you only need about 20 – 40 minutes of medication daily.

To practice effective medication for memory improvement, you would need to engage in the following routines;

    i. When you are awake in the morning, try to recap the activities you carried out from the morning of the previous day until the hour that you fell asleep for about 20 minutes.

    ii. In the evening before going to bed, take about 30 minutes to meditate and think about the major activities you carried out during the day.

These two processes listed above, will help to improve your ability to recall information, retain them and remember them when needed.

The benefits of meditation

i. Thickens your cerebral cortex (brain outer layer)

ii. It improves concentration

Factors that improve memory:

(1) **Healthy Eating:** A Mediterranean diet helps to provide vital nutrients needed by our brain to function. Learn more about food that improves memory in chapter five (5).

(2) **Exercise:** Physical exercise can help to build a strong body and healthy heart. Aerobic exercises are found to be good for memory improvement.

(3) **Mineral supplements and vitamins:** Supplements from vitamin C & D has been known to be of great benefits in memory formation and retrieval of important information.

(4) **Mental Activities:** Playing games like Chess, Puzzle cards, UNO, or Go fish, can help in having better and stronger memory.

(5) Avoid stress

(6) **Make a To-Do list**.

FACTORS THAT CONTRIBUTE TO MEMORY LOSS

It is important to note that, there are different factors that contribute to poor memory or memory loss in the worst case: Below are some of the common factors.

(1) **Inactivity:** It is a natural law that whatever is not in use depreciates. Hence, any memory that is not fully used

for the purpose of storing, retrieving and processing information begins to depreciate.

(2) **Sickness and Diseases:** Chronic illnesses have the ability to damage one's memory. Hence, proper treatment for sickness and diseases is recommended by healthcare providers.

(3) **Attitude and Behavior:** Anxiety, fear, and negative self image can sometimes result to poor memory. People who are in continuous self-doubt always have poor memory.

(4) **Medications:** Side effects from drugs can sometimes lead to poor memory and memory loss.

(5) **Alcohol:** Heavy consumption of alcohol can lead to memory impairment.

(6) **Depression and Emotional Problems:** Depression can make us to lose focus and concentration. Thereby leading to poor memory or memory loss.

(7) **Grief and Death:** Losing someone close to us, can cause pains, grief and sometimes memory loss. As we regain consciousness, our memory functions return to normal state.

SOME COMMON REASONS WHY SOME TEENS AND YOUNG ADULTS PERFORM POOR IN EXAMINATIONS

1. **PROCRASTINATION:** This is a characteristic that is found common amongst students. In this modern and digital world where teenager spend hours chatting with friends on Facebook, Twitter, Snapchat and other social platforms, many seems to have little or

no time for their academic activities. To many, the future seems far away than it truly is. They allow short term activities to overwhelm their long-term objectives. Instead of reading their notes at the beginning of a semester, they tend to keep it further towards the end of the semester. They can go to cinema house on Wednesday night for movies; dinner night on Thursday, party on Friday, and football show on Saturday so on and so forth. They often carry out this same behavior next week, and the week after that until it is few days to examinations, where they begin to stock pile everything in their memory, forgetting that their brain isn't a magic pot. To avoid this situation, there is need to prepare yourself early for the semester ahead.

2.   **SLEEP:** Teenagers and young adults do not always have enough hours of sleep at night. It is not because they are deprived of it, simply put, - due to adolescents and young adult lifestyle. Teenagers can stay awake all through the night chatting with friends far away in other continents like Europe, Asia and Africa without feeling bored. But most of them cannot spend three (3) hours to study and revise what they have been taught. This is another

cause of poor performance amongst teens during examination. To avoid this temptation, it is advisable that you disconnect your internet service at night when studying or before going to bed.

VISUALIZATION AND IMAGINATION

There is not much difference between visualization and imagination, as these two components are often used interchangeably.

VISUALIZATION

Visualization is about forming mental image of a situation in our brain based on previous knowledge which might be true. If you ask your kids, what they would like to be in the future? Automatically, they will use their power of visualization to answer you based on what they have recorded in their memory. It could be things they have seen, heard, or read. One would say, I want to be a doctor, the other would say, I want to be a pilot; the other one would say I want to be a policeman. If you ask further, how do you plan to accomplish this? They will also use the power of visualization to explain to you or tell you a story on how they wish to get it done. Funny enough, their instincts might be right or wrong. But they just simply tell you the future based on the mental pictures recorded in their brain. I love it when I hear my little boy say to me "daddy I will buy you a BIG car". It simply shows, he is able to form a mental picture of things he has seen on the TV, road or in his computer game.

IMAGINATION

Imagination is also a strong mental exercise that can help to improve our memory. It can help us to form a mental image of things we have never seen, or heard without placing limit to our ability to achieve them. Your imagination may not always be true, but no one is going to punish you for aiming so high in your imagination. Therefore you are free to use your imagination to visualize your future. Most people had never been to the USA physically, but they have been here (US) severally via imagination to meet with – Mr. President, go to beautiful places, have good times with celebrities and other stuffs like that – All thanks to their power of imagination. This is something that would have cost them money and time in real life, but they just simply got it done free of charge through imagination.

So, you can imagine anything and be in anywhere through imagination, but don't travel too far, remember to come back to reality. As student, you can imagine scoring first in your next exams. As teenagers, you can imagine being the next president of the USA. But you must remember the need to work hard to make your imagination a reality. Every dream or goal achieved is a product of imagination. Hence, do not limit your power of imagination, because *"whether you think you can or you cannot, you are always right"* Henry Ford.

CHAPTER FOUR

HOW TO DEVELOP DISCIPLINE

TO PRACTICE MEMORY

IMPROVEMENT

In other to bring out the creativity in you and
also to improve your memory; you need to
apply discipline to your life. There is a regular

saying that, "*The more you do what you have been doing, the more you will get what you have been getting.*" In the quest for memory improvement, self discipline is an essential requirement. You will need discipline to practice meditation, mental exercise, mind mapping, physical exercise, mind shift and so on.

To develop high level of discipline as a teen or young adult, you will need to poses the "habits of highly effective people".

Scott Berkun in **The myths of innovation** pointed out these "seven habits of highly innovative people".

1. **Persistence:** Innovation requires more than great ideas. It requires faith, action, persistence and hard work. These four points are needed to have an improved memory.

2. **Remove self-limitation/inhibition:** To have improved and better memory, you need to break self-imposed limitations and learn new skills believing that you can learn and become perfect at any new task. Is it learning how to speak French, play the piano, play scrabble and chess games, etc?

3. **Take risk and make mistake:** While learning a new task, do not be

afraid of failure because it is often associated with learning. If you have never failed, you have never learned.

4. **Escape: Find out your most creative movement**. When is that moment in your life, where you feel so excited and energetic? For me, it usually happens in the morning, few minutes after I have woken up or late in the night when I am alone. I also feel excited when playing slow music (blues) while reading or studying something new. So, you can find out your best moment and convert it to your peak hour.

5. **Writing things down:** Highly creative people have always learned to write something down. Be it on papers, jotters, dairy, or in the form of sketch. This will help you to recall information easily when needed.

6. **Find patterns and create combination:** You can improve your memory by being exposed and building on ideas or things you already know. If you already know that reading journals and current affairs can improve your memory, then go further by reading other materials that may also contribute to memory improvement.

7. **Curiosity:** Most innovators and creative people are curious and have a strong desire to solve problems. As a teenager or young adult, think of problems you can solve to engage in memory test. Are there things needed by your fellow students that will make their lives pretty much easy and comfortable? Can you come up with an app game to solve people's problem? Because adolescent and young adults are more interested in playing app games than people in their age 30s, 40s and above.

COMMON FACTORS THAT AFFECT CREATIVE THINKING

A Harvard Professor, Teresa Amabile listed the followings as factors that can affect creative thinking:

i. **Discouragement:** In your quest to being creative, be ready to accept criticism from friends and family members who would never support or believe in your creative ability. It wasn't easy for Steve Job (founder of Apple computers); neither did it come easy for everyone to believe in Bill Gate, It wasn't also a fun ride at the beginning for Mark Zuckerberg (Owner of Facebook). But today, these gentlemen had registered their names in the hall of fame. Therefore, don't throw in the towel because of criticism. Believe that you can develop your skills and be the best in your field.

ii. **Negative feedback:** Positive feedback and praise can help you to become more creative, but some people aren't that nice always to give you that little support you needed from them. Again, be prepared for some negative comments.

iii. **Role mismatch:** This happens when you are assigned to projects you have little or no interest in. Although you might gain some level of experience, but your creativity becomes restricted due to lack of interest.

iv. **Too much end-goal restriction:** When involved in group work/project, individuals should be allowed to contribute their ideas.

How to Lose Inhibition as

Teenage/Young Adult

1. **Think to React:** Do you always see yourself as a low-class person amongst your friends? Do you feel shy to raise hand and provide answer to question(s) in the class or in any social gathering? If this is your case, you might be limiting your brain power to shyness or self imposed limitations. Whenever this occurs, think quickly and react positively to the challenge.

2. **Face the situation:** As a teenager, if inhibition hinders you from exploring your full potentials, sit and analyze the situation that makes you feel timid. By using your brain power to brainstorm or meditate on the condition for 20 – 45 minutes, you will develop the best way to defeat inhibition.

3. **Be proud of who you are:** Teenagers, who often feel timid, are isolated, have negative self-belief, and low self-esteem. They feel apprehensive and are exposed to poor memory or memory loss condition. React to every situation in your best way. Feel happy

always, have fun with friends, associate with both sex (male/female), and think less about your body image if there is anything to bother about.

4. **Participate in Group Activities:** The more you openly associate with friends, the more you overcome fear and inhibition. Just do some funny and crazy things occasionally to surprise your friends. If you are called out in a friend's party, feel excited to show some dancing steps even if you can't do it like Usher-Raymond or Beyonce.

5. **Set limit for your actions:** The fact that you want to lose inhibition is not a

call to engage in "social vices". Hence,

introduce some level of discipline to your

actions. Note that you are accountable for

your actions wherever you are.

CHAPTER FIVE

HOW TO USE DIETS TO

IMPROVE MEMORY

According to Sarah Mahoney in Brain foods your kids need *"for years, athletes have eaten to win. It is also possible for kids to eat to learn"*. The importance of healthy eating and brain diets cannot be overemphasized for memory improvement. The following food will help to keep your brain and memory at mental alert.

1. **Coconut oil:** Has been known to support healthy heart, lower high blood pressure and stabilize blood sugar level.

2. **Blueberries:** It helps to protect the brain against oxidative damage and stress.

3. **Dark chocolate:** Contains antioxidants, help to improve mood, blood vessel function and memory.

4. **Quinoa:** It contains good carbohydrate and fiber that helps to balance blood sugar.

5. **Rosemary:** It helps to improve mood, blood flow to the brain, improves memory, boost energy and serve as an anti-aging for skin.

6. **Avocados:** Avocados is a major source of good and healthy fat like omega 3 and omega 6 fatty acid. Avocados are known to lower cholesterol, increase blood flow to the brain, contain vitamin E and K that help to protect the brain against partial or severe stroke.

7. **Bean and legumes:** Are good sources of complex carbohydrate and fiber that help to supply glucose to the brain. They are also rich in omega fatty acid and

Folate (an essential vitamin B needed by the brain).

8. **Broccoli:** Is very rich in Iron, calcium, vitamin K, B. vitamins, vitamin C and betacarotene. These nutrients help improve blood flow to the brain, and also remove heavy metal that can cause damage to the brain.

9. **Nuts:** Walnuts and almonds are known to contain good sources of omega 3 and omega 6 fatty acid – essential nutrients for the brain and nervous system. They also contain vitamin E and vitamin B6.

10. **Spinach:** Spinach can help to fight against tumor growth, brain cancer, and aging.

11. **Whole grains:** Whole grain is known to contain healthy carbohydrate, omega 3 fatty acid, fiber, and B vitamins. These nutrients help to protect the heart and brain against any form of damage caused by blood clots, cholesterol and sugar spikes.

12. **Water:** The brain is made up of about 75% water. Hence dehydration can lead to brain shrinkage, poor memory or temporary memory loss.

13. **Fish:** Salmon fish is known to contain low fat. Regular consumption of salmon fish is known to improve memory and thinking ability amongst teens. The Rush University Medical study reported by MSNBC, states that "a diet that contained at least one source of fish per week improves people's memory and thinking ability when compared to people who did not eat fish.

14. **Apples:** Consumption of an apple per day can help to improve focus, study habits and academic performance amongst school children. The peel of the

apple contains antioxidant that helps to improve memory.

15. **Onions:** Inclusion of onions in our diet can help to improve memory and focus. It also has the ability to prevent Alzheimer's disease.

16. **Coffee:** Coffee is the number one brain booster substance. Consumption of coffee can help to improve memory, boost mood, and increase overall brain function.

17. **Yerbal mate:** Yerbal mate is a tea brewed from the South America. It helps to increase mental focus, clarity and energy.

18. **Green tea:** Green tea contain an important amino acid (L-theanine) that helps to improve learning, boost mood and improve one's ability to recall information.

19. **Curry:** The Curcumin contained in curry makes it vital nutrient for the brain and memory function.

20. **Egg:** Egg contains Choline an important vitamin-like substance for the creation of memory stem cells. Also diets that is rich in Choline helps adolescent to remember things better and helps in the production of new memory cell in childhood and adulthood.

21. **Whole Wheat:** Whole wheat breads are rich in Folate and B vitamins for the production of new memory and brain cells.

22. **Cereal:** Cereal is rich in Folate, complex carbohydrates, protein and vitamin B12 that help out brain to remember things or past events.

23. **Milk:** Unsaturated and fat-free milk contain phosphorus, protein and vitamin D which help to improve your brain function and improves memory.

24. **Fruit:** Fiber rich fruits-like, pears, apples, melons, plums and oranges are

known to enhance our energy level and also improve the brain overall functions.

25. **Chia:** Chia seeds help to control blood sugar level, increase hydration and also serve as antioxidants. Chia seeds contain omega 3 fatty acid and soluble and insoluble fiber.

CONCLUSION

The aim of this book is to help our kids, teens and young adults have improved memory, become more active and responsible in the society, develop personal discipline, improve in academic performance, and to realize the possibility of training our brain to learn new things, process new information and recall them when needed.

"Whether you think you can or you think you cannot, you are always right,"- Henry Ford.

Thanks for downloading and reading a copy of this book. I hope you have learned one or two things. If truly, you've found this book helpful, order an extra copy for a friend, family member, associate or school mates. Your honest review for this book will be highly appreciated. Please drop your comment and review at the review section in amazon.com.

Scott Lewis.

REFERENCES

1. 6Brain Training Exercise for Children and Teens. Dr Robert Myers, PhD

2. 8 Working Memory Boosters. Amanda Morin

3. 10 Ways to Boost Your Memory (Daily mail). Angela Epstein

4. Memory Development In Teenagers. Koujln

5. Developing your Ability to Remember (Veer). Ellis Bronte.

6. 20 Study Hacks to Improve Your Memory. Andrea Leyden.

Made in the USA
San Bernardino, CA
13 December 2018